Thaddeus Amat

A treatise on matrimony, according to the doctrine and discipline of the Catholic Church

Thaddeus Amat

A treatise on matrimony, according to the doctrine and discipline of the Catholic Church

ISBN/EAN: 9783337261771

Printed in Europe, USA, Canada, Australia, Japan

Cover: Foto ©Lupo / pixelio.de

More available books at **www.hansebooks.com**

A

TREATISE ON MATRIMONY,

ACCORDING TO THE

DOCTRINE AND DISCIPLINE

OF THE

CATHOLIC CHURCH.

BY RT. REV'D DOCTOR AMAT,
BISHOP OF MONTEREY, CALIFORNIA.

SAN FRANCISCO:
PUBLISHED BY MICHAEL FLOOD, 428 KEARNY ST.
Towne & Bacon, Printers, 536 Clay Street.
1864.

TREATISE ON MATRIMONY.

MATRIMONY, one of the institutions of God himself
from the beginning of the world, for the preservation
of the human race, created after his own image and
likeness, was to bear the stamp of the divine goodness,
which the Supreme Architect had impressed on all his
works; "and God saw all the things that he had made,
and they were very good." (Gen. c. 15, v. 31); and
being designed, as we learn from the great Apostle, to
symbolize that admirable union which was to be effected in the fullness of time, by the infinite charity of God,
of the divine and human nature in the Person of the
Eternal Word, incarnate; and of the Eternal Word
incarnate, Jesus Christ, with all the members of the
human race, engrafted in Him by the grace of regene-
ration, namely the Church; it was necessary that it
should have also the stamp of unity and perpetuity,
grounded on charity and love, superior even to that
which man owes to his progenitors : " For this cause,
thus speaks the above cited Apostle (Eph. c. 5, vv. 31,
32), shall a man leave his father and mother, and shall
cleave to his wife, and they shall be two in one flesh :
This is a great sacrament; but I speak in Christ and
in the Church." Hence Matrimony, from the very beginning of creation, was a sacred sign, although not a

sacrament, a dignity which was reserved for the time of the Christian Dispensation; it was a sacred sign of the most sacred and admirable union of Jesus Christ with his Church, and of the grace which was to be conferred by Christian marriage under the new dispensation. As the ancient sacrifices had no virtue of their own, but through the sacrifice of Jesus Christ, which they promised and of which they were a figure; they were as "a shadow of the good things to come" (Heb. c. 10, v. 1), as St. Paul says, so also matrimony amongst our forefathers was a figure of the Christian marriage, and of the grace which was to be annexed to the same by our Lord Jesus Christ, in order that those engaged in the matrimonial state, under the perfect law of the gospel, which is a law of charity, might more fully represent the union of Christ with the Church, and raise up their children in the love and fear of God, and obedience to Jesus Christ.

Hence, matrimony can be considered under two different aspects: as a contract, and as a sacrament. As a contract established by God himself from the beginning; and as a sacrament of the new law, established by Jesus Christ—these two qualities being inseparable in the Christian marriage, since it is the same matrimonial contract, established by God from the beginning, which our divine Saviour raised to the dignity of a sacrament for all those who have received the Christian baptism. On the knowledge of the matrimonial contract greatly depends the right understanding of the same as a sacrament—the object we have in view by these few lines, for the benefit of our Catholic friends.

Although matrimony, as we shall see, is a mutually

onerous contract between man and woman; and on this account it might be as well called patrimony as matrimony, which means—the duty both of father and mother (*Patris vel Matris munus*)—still as it is much more onerous and laborious to the woman, to whom it belongs to conceive, bring forth, and train up her offspring, it is for this reason called, more appropriately, "matrimony." It is likewise called "wedlock" (*conjugium*), from the conjugal union of man and wife, united, as it were, by a common yoke, and mutually bound to each other. Matrimony can be defined thus: "The conjugal and legitimate union of man and woman, which is to last during life." The word "union" expresses the mutual tie and obligation by which the man and woman are bound to each other; that of "conjugal" indicates the peculiar character of this union, binding their own persons to each other, which distinguishes the matrimonial contract from all others; "legitimate," this word not only means that said union is honest and lawful, but also that it is to be contracted under certain laws; the words "which is to last during life," express the indissolubility of the tie which binds husband and wife.

Matrimony is a natural contract established by God from the beginning of creation; hence we read in the first chapter of the book of Genesis (vv. 27, 28), that "God created man to his own image . . . . . male and female he created them;" and again, "God blessed them, saying, increase and multiply," which words by no means imply a precept for all to marry, as some erroneously interpret them, as we shall see hereafter; but they merely express the object of matrimony, the propagation of the human race, for which purpose he had made them male and female, and rendered them fruitful by his blessing. In the second chapter of the same book, we learn the secondary object of the matrimonial contract, as intended by God, namely, the mutual comfort and assistance of husband and wife, their domestic felicity, as comprised in these words which God said: "It is not good for man to be alone, let us make him a help like unto himself" (v. 18); and having formed the first woman out of one of the ribs of Adam, by which God intended to teach them, that they were to treat each other as companions and not as servants, God brought the woman to Adam, "And Adam said, this now is bone of my bones, and flesh of my flesh; she shall be called woman, because she was taken out of man; wherefore a man shall leave father and mother, and shall cleave to his wife, and they shall be two in one flesh" (vv. 23, 24). That these words, although pronounced by the first parent of the human race, were pronounced by God's authority establishing matrimony, is authoritatively declared by our Lord Jesus Christ, answering the question proposed to him by the Pharisees, whether "it were lawful for a man to put away his wife for every cause; he answered and said to them, have ye not read, that he who made man in the beginning, made them male and female? and he said, for this cause shall a man leave father and mother, and shall cleave unto his wife; and they two shall be in one flesh; wherefore they are no more two, but one flesh. What therefore God hath joined together, let not man put asunder." (Matt. c. 19, v. 3, etc.)

This matrimonial contract, having the seal of God's authority, the Supreme Author of nature, and being according to the end which he proposed to himself in the formation of the two first parents of the human race, even before their prevarication, could not be but good and holy; contrary to the teaching of those ancient heretics, who, as Saint Paul says, writing to his disciple Timothy, departed "from the faith, giving heed to spirits of error, and doctrines of devils," and "forbidding to marry," (First Tim. ch. 4, v. 1, and following,) as coming from an evil principle. This monstrous doctrine needs no confutation, since it is evident by the very words of its institution, that matrimony was established by the Almighty for the purpose of preventing the promiscuous intercourse of the sexes in the procreation of children, for promoting domestic felicity, and for securing the maintenance and education of children; all of which is well protected by its unity and indissolubility, being "two in one flesh," and placed out of the reach of man to dissolve the union; "what God hath joined together, let not man put asunder."

Such was the matrimonial contract—from the beginning, one and indissoluble; and being such by divine institution, it was held in great veneration amongst all nations, to which the knowledge of its divine origin had reached by oral tradition from the first parents of the human race, to whom, the union of Jesus Christ with his Church, by which, as the Apostle says: (Eph. ch. 5, v. 31) "we are members of his body, of his flesh and of his bones," and which is represented by the matrimonial contract, was made manifest by divine light when he took for his wife the first woman whom he called "bone of his bones, and flesh of his flesh." Hence, before the coming of Christ our Lord, no human legislator ever dared to touch, with profane hands, the matrimonial contract, but it was left altogether under the control of religion, whose ceremonies ordinarily accompanied its celebration ; such was the case among the Persians, Egyptians, Greeks, and Romans; they considered and held matrimony as a sacred thing, and used to call it "a communication of the divine and human right," and the woman by it was said to be "partaker of sacred things." Human legislation cannot loose the ties that bind the offspring to their parents; much less could it dissolve the conjugal union, far superior to the first, since by it the first is dissolved. "A man shall leave father and mother, and shall cleave to his wife." How could the human legislator separate two persons united into one and the same flesh? "And they shall be two in one flesh." No; "what God hath joined together let not man put asunder."

By what has been said, it appears evident that matrimony, as an institution of God, is one, holy and indissoluble; or has three essential conditions: Unity, Sanctity, and Indissolubility. Unity: they are not two, but "one flesh." Sanctity : representing the union of Jesus Christ with his church; and Indissolubility: "what God hath joined together, let not man put asunder." Unity condemns polygamy, or the plurality of wives, against the practice of Mormonism. Sanctity condemns all those who look upon matrimony as a mere civil contract, and treat it as such. And Indissolubility condemns divorce, as coming from Judaism. We therefore proceed now to the consideration of these three different errors, as we consider them in opposition to the nature of the matrimonial contract according to God's institution.

Although polygamy be contrary to the matrimonial contract, as established by the Creator, who made it one, as we have said; and although even it be not conducive to the secondary end of matrimony, which is, as we have seen, domestic felicity, no one can doubt, however, that God can dispense with it, since it is not contrary to the first and principal object of matrimony, the procreation of children; and if any shadow of doubt should remain on the subject, it would be easily removed by the fact that God granted such dispensation to several of the patriarchs, as Abraham, Jacob, and David, as it can be seen in the Holy Scriptures (Gen. c. 16: 29, 30, and Second Kings, c. 5); for we could not consistently with the Holy Word of God, sustain the sanctity of those holy fathers, but by supposing the divine dispensation of a law which by no means could be unknown to them. Such being the case, it would be temerity for us to ask the reason why God granted such dispensation. We know it was done for the most wise reasons, entering into the designs of his divine providence, foreshadowing something mysterious of the union of Jesus Christ with his church, always represented by matrimony: perhaps the plurality of nations and tribes, called and united into one and the same church, one and the same faith, by christian baptism, through Jesus Christ, whom the patriarch also prefigured. Such was the opinion of Saint Augustin, saying (*De bono conjug.* c. 18, v. 21), " plures uxores antiqurum Patrum significaverunt puturas nostras ex omnibus gentibus ecclesias, uni viro subditas Christo." He might also have granted such dispensation to the patriarchs, his faithful servants, for the purpose of increasing the num-

1*

ber of his true adorers in a time when idolatry was so widely spread over the world that few only, comparatively, knew and worshiped the true God.

There are plausible reasons for granting said dispensation, which, however, could never be applied to the plurality of husbands, never granted by Almighty God, as being contrary to all and each of the ends of matrimony, especially to the first, the propagation of children. These reasons having ceased by the coming of the Divine Redeemer, and the establishment of one spiritual kingdom over the world, by the preaching of His doctrine, we can see no cause why polygamy should have been allowed under the christian dispensation, and not rather abolished, and matrimony restored to its first unity, namely: that of "one man with one woman," representing the union of Jesus Christ with his Church, formed out of all nations; thus thought also the aforesaid Father, (loc. cit.), "Onius uxoris vir significat ex omnibus gentibus unitatem uni viro subditam Christo;" and "therefore," continues Saint Augustine (same place), "as the mystery of several wives anciently signified the future multitude of all earthly nations that were to be subjected to God: so also in our days, the mystery of one wife with one husband represents the unity of us all subject to God to be perfected in one heavenly city." However, whatever may be the reasons against polygamy and in favor of the unity of matrimony, it is certain that Jesus Christ, the true Legislator of mankind, to whom all power was given by his Eternal Father (Matt. c. 28, v. 18), and whom we are commanded to obey (Luke c. 9, v. 35), abolished polygamy or the plurality of wives, under the christian dispensation; restored matrimony to its primitive unity, such as it was established by God in the beginning, and declared the matrimonial engagement, whether made by male or female, whilst a previous one exists, although the dissolution of the first may be pretended by virtue of a divorce, to be but an adulterous union, and by no means a lawful matrimony: " From the beginning of the creation," says he, " God made them male and female; for this cause a man shall leave his father and mother, and shall cleave to his wife, and they two shall be one flesh," and " whosoever shall put away his wife, and marry another, committeth adultery. * * And if the wife shall put away her husband, and be married to another, she committeth adultery." (Mark, c. 10, vv. 6,—8, 11, 12.) Such is the standard law of Jesus Christ, the Supreme Legislator of mankind, binding all men, whether Jews or Gentiles; condemning by it polygamy, and every kind of Mormonism of the past, present and future time, and rendering null and void every human law in opposition to his.

Matrimony, as we have seen, is a natural contract, sanctioned by divine authority, for the procreation of children and preservation of society; this is its primary object; and on this account it is evident that society is greatly interested in its rightful celebration. Its secondary object being to promote domestic felicity, the happiness and comfort of the family, on which greatly depends the well-being of society at large and the prosperity of nations, since it is the collection or aggregation of such that forms the nation and greatly affects it, especially with regard to legitimacy, and the right of inheritance. Therefore civil rulers are bound to protect it by wise laws, and to preserve always the sanctity of the matrimonial contract, according to God's institution· Hence comes the distinction between natural and civil contract, religious and political engagement. Hence the zeal of civil magistrates and legislators in enacting laws regulating marriages or the matrimonial contract; and hence, too, the error of those, whether civil magistrates, legislators, or the common people, who, regardless of the laws of God and of religion, call matrimony and hold it as a a mere civil contract, treating it as any other contract or transaction under their exclusive jurisdiction, enacting laws affecting its validity or invalidity, and pronouncing decrees of divorce or dissolution of the ties of matrimony, granting leave to marry or to be married to another; all of which can never make good what God has invalidated, or dissolve what God has united, since there is no power against the power of God, who established matrimony one and indissoluble: "a man shall leave father and mother and shall cleave to his wife, and they two shall be one flesh; wherefore they are no more two, but one flesh;" and he has withdrawn from men the faculty of altering it: "what God hath joined together let not man put asunder."

Matrimony, as a natural contract, being established by God from the beginning, for the objects above said, is anterior to all society; and restored by Jesus Christ under the Christian Dispensation, to its primitive institution as to its essential qualities, and placed out of the reach of man to alter it, as we have already established, it becomes evident that the civil contract of matrimony, if there be any, is posterior to the natural one, nor can it affect by any means, God's institution. Therefore, the nature of the civil contract of matrimony can only extend to and have only civil effects, leaving untouched the natural contract. It is something adventitious, not inherent to matrimony, which was perfect as coming from the Creator, and for ages in existance before the civil contract was known; and it is still perfect to-day without any civil contract whenever there are no civil laws regarding matrimony, as it is in several countries, and also amongst tribes uncivilized; and as valid as to the matrimonial contract as it can be under the most refined civil legislation. We by no means, however, pretend to deny to civil legislators the faculty of enacting laws concerning marriage, since from it proceed, as we have already said, rights and duties which fall under the control of civil magistrates, and consequently must of necessity be regulated by wise civil laws, which we said shall produce their civil effects, and bind the citizens. But moreover, bound as they are, to protect by wise laws the rights of citizens, the eternal laws of justice and public morality which corrupt people are too apt to violate, unless restrained through the fear of them who, as Saint Paul says (Rom. c. 13, v. 4) : bear "not the sword in vain," being the ministers of God and avengers " to execute wrath upon " them that do "evil:" so they are not less bound to protect matrimony, as an institution of God, to secure its essential qualities, especially in a country where every system of religion being authorized, or at least tolerated, by law, the corruption of the human heart and its untamed passions are apt to introduce, under the pretext of religion, to the prejudice of public and even common decency, the most infamous crimes and abominations, as is testified by the history of humanity.

Let, then, human legislators, in enacting laws concerning marriage, be careful not to extend their legis-
lative power beyond the civil power confided to their
care ; directing well, according to the rights of eternal
justice, the effects resulting from the matrimonial contract, inasmuch as they may affect civil order or the
order of society ; and leave sacred and untouched the
matrimonial contract itself, as an institution of God ;
and their laws will be by all respected. But if they
go beyond that, their laws shall command neither respect nor esteem, nor even obedience, whenever peo_
ple will be able to evade them. Let them not yield,
in the formation of their laws, to the depraved inclinations of the human heart, which would bring them to
legalize the most brutal passions, without satisfying
them ; but rather enforce by wise laws the essential
conditions of the matrimonial contract established by
the Creator of mankind for the preservation and perfection of human society, and thus they will effectually
coöperate to its enlightenment and to the preservation
of the image and likeness of God, which we bear in our
souls and distinguishes us from the brute creation.

Having thus briefly explained our candid views concerning polygamy, and the error of such as look upon
matrimony as a mere civil contract, as being opposed
both to the union and sanctity of the matrimonial
engagement, it remains for us to show how divorce also
is opposed to its indissolubility or perpetuity.

Every one can easily understand that although the
primary object of the matrimonial contract, the procreation of children, demands not its perpetuity, since
they could be obtained with only a temporary contract ;

still the proper training of the same, their education, the noblest part of the same primary object, as also the secondary one, namely, domestic peace and felicity, resulting from love, uniting the parents amongst themselves and the offspring to their parents, cannot be secured without the perpetual tie that binds the couple to each other ; and since God made all things good from the beginning, and He made the first man perfect, and destined his children to be taught by the parents, and thus be conducted to perfection, He must have made the matrimonial tie perpetual, or else He would not have sufficiently provided for the object He had in view. Whether He could dispense with it, we will not venture to ask ; since He could have even established the matrimonial tie temporal, providing some other means for the proper education of children, so He could dispense with the law which He himself had made, and allow its dissolution, as He really did, granting to the •Jews, for certain reasons, the faculty of giving the bill of divorce, remaining free after that to marry another. But Jesus Christ abolished said permission under the Christian dispensation, and restored matrimony to its primitive institution, rendering it perpetual and indissoluble ; answering to the Jews who justified themselves in the practice of putting away their wives, alleging the law of Moses which "permitted" to write a bill of divorce and to put them away, Jesus said to them, " Because of the hardness of your heart he wrote you, that precept; but from the beginning of the creation God made them male and female ; for this cause a man shall leave his father and mother, and shall cleave to his wife, and they two shall be one flesh. What, there-

fore, God hath joined together, let no man put asunder."
And immediately after, speaking to his disciples concerning the same thing, He said to them : " Whosoever
shall put away his wife and marry another, committeth
adultery against her ; and if the wife shall put away
her husband and be married to another, she committeth
adultery." (Mark, c. 10, vv. 4–12.)

This is the standard law of Jesus Christ under the
Christian dispensation, binding all men, whether Christians, Jews, or Gentiles ; a law superior to all human
laws ; which no human law can ever destroy, and
which annuls all laws against it, from whatever authority they may proceed and by whatever magistrate they
may be enacted, whatever may be the opinions of men
to the contrary, since there is no power against the
power of God : " what God hath joined together, let no
man put asunder." Let civil magistrates grant divorces
of marriages previously legally contracted ; let them
exercise this power as long as they please, they can
never prescribe against the law of God declaring matrimony to be one and indissoluble. They may grant to
the couple divorced the faculty of marrying again, and
declare the second engagement valid according to the
civil law ; but according to the law of God and the gospel, it shall always be an unlawful union and a real
adultery : " Whosoever shall put away his wife and
marry another, committeth adultery ; and if the wife
shall put away her husband and be married to another,
she committeth adultery."

We have elsewhere said, that the matrimonial contract, from its first institution, was a holy, a sacred
thing ; not only on account of its divine origin, but

moreover on account of its being designed to represent that admirable union which was to be effected in the fullness of time between Jesus Christ and his Church. There is nothing in matrimony so strikingly representative of this union as its perpetuity and indissolubility; for the human flesh which the Eternal Word assumed for the redemption of mankind He shall never abandon, as is beautifully expressed by Saint John, saying, "And the Word was made flesh, and dwelt amongst us" (c. 1, v. 14); and the same He assumed in heaven at the right hand of his Eternal Father. This is the reason why Jesus Christ did not allow any longer divorce under the Christian dispensation, restoring matrimony to its primitive purity, and rendering its tie indissoluble.

We have considered matrimony so far under the aspect of a natural contract, established by God from the beginning, one, holy, and indissoluble; excluding equally polygamy and divorce, and condemning such as would consider it as a mere civil contract, depriving it of the sacredness attached to it by the Almighty. We proceed now to consider the same as a sacrament of the new law established by our Lord Jesus Christ for all who have received Christian baptism.

That matrimony, under the Christian dispensation, or the matrimonial contract between two baptized and faithful Christians, be one of the seven sacraments established by our Lord Jesus Christ, which He left in the Church for the sanctification of its members, is one of the dogmas of the Christian faith and of divine revelation, constantly held in the Church, sustained by the Fathers, expressed in the rituals, and believed by the faithful; and thus defined against the Reformers by the

General Council of Trent: "If any one say that matrimony is not verily and properly one of the seven sacraments of the evangelical law instituted by Christ our Lord, let him be anathema." (Can. 1, Sec. 24.) Not only did our divine Saviour honor matrimony as an institution of God by his presence at the marriage feast of Cana in Galilee (John, c. 2), and sanctified it by his first miracle changing water into wine, condemning thus by his conduct such as were afterwards "giving heed to doctrines of devils," as we observed before, forbidding marriage as an unlawful deed; but, moreover, He confirmed by his authority the unity and indissolubility of the matrimonial tie, condemning polygamy and divorce against the Mormon and Jewish practice (Matt. 19 and Mark 10), as we have already proved; and this matrimonial tie, a mere figure of the union of Jesus Christ with his Church before his incarnation, He rendered productive of divine grace, through his passion and death, for the sanctification of the contracting parties, as He also sanctified his Church; and thus enabled them to fulfill those supernatural duties resulting from Christian marriage—duties which could not be duly complied with unless by a special and supernatural grace, which grace God will not refuse; and has consequently annexed it to this sacrament, as the Church has formally declared as an article of divine faith: "If any one say that matrimony . . . does not confer grace, let him be anathema." (Can. 1, Sec. 24.)

From this principle of divine faith, that matrimony, or the matrimonial contract, amongst Christians, is a sacrament, and that it confers sanctifying grace, it follows as a necessary consequence, that it is a sacred thing of a supernatural order, whose management and administration belongs to the church and its ministers, they being, according to the doctrine of Saint Paul, " the ministers of Christ, and the dispensers of the mysteries of God." (1st Cor. c. 4.) And this is precisely what the church, in the Council of Trent, decided, when she said (Can. 11, Sec. 24) : " If any one say that the matrimonial causes do not belong to the ecclesiastical judges, let him be anathema." To the church, then, it belongs to regulate the Christian matrimony, or the marriage of those who profess the Christian faith and belong to the church, having received Christian baptism ; such marriage, as we have said, being a sacrament, and being the same matrimonial contract which God established from the beginning, which our Saviour raised to the dignity of a sacrament, attaching to it sanctifying grace. Hence it has been confided to the church and placed under her protection, and therefore to the church belongs to regulate, by wise laws, the marriage contract amongst Christians ; so that on the observance of said laws will depend the lawfulness and validity of the matrimonial tie. This has also been defined by the church as an article of faith, condemning as heretics such as would deny to her the faculty, or would dare to affirm that she has erred in exercising the same, saying: "If any one say that the church cannot establish impediments annulling matrimony, or that she has erred in establishing them, let him be anathema." (Can. 4, Sec. 24.)

These few points, on which depends all that we are to say, or can say, concerning Christian marriage, being decided upon by the infallible authority of the church, against which the gates of hell shall never prevail (Matt. c. 16, v. 18), and which, being "the pillar and ground of the truth (1 Tim. c. 3, v. 15), we are commanded by our Lord to obey, even as himself (Luke c. 10, v. 16), we can say, with full confidence, that we are placed on solid ground, independently of any other proof from Holy writ; but they have, besides, for their support, the doctrine and practice of the great Apostle Paul, who has written the first code of legislation, by which the church has been guided in matrimonial concerns. In the fifth chapter of his Epistle to the Ephesians, Saint Paul draws a line of comparison between matrimony and the union of Jesus Christ with the church, of which it has always been a figure—the husband being the head of the wife, as Christ is the head of the church; and the members of the church, which is the body of Christ, being therefore "the members of his body, of his flesh, and of his bones," as the first woman, taken out of Adam, was said to be "bone of his bone, and flesh of his flesh." He extols the Christian marriage above the ancient one, although the same established by God from the beginning, by the superiority of duties resulting from it, such as supernatural love and respect for one another, similar to that which exists between Christ and his church, implying a special grace attached to the same to sanctify the contracting parties, as Christ sanctified the Church, by virtue of which he calls it "a great Sacrament in Christ and in the church;" and therefore as a sacred thing, as a Minister of Christ, and Dispenser of the mysteries of God, he knew he had authority to regulate the marriage contract amongst Christians, as he did in many instances, especially in the seventh chapter of the first Epistle to the Corinthians, which would have been in itself sufficient guaranty for the church to decide upon her power to regulate by wise laws the matrimonial contract amongst Christians, as we have established above.

The church, then, of her own authority, that is to say, independently of any civil power or magistrate, but only by virtue of the power she received from her Divine founder, can enact laws concerning Christian marriages, regulating their contract, and affecting their lawfulness and validity, which no other laws can do, by whatever magistrate or authority they may be enacted, unless approved and sanctioned by the same. Civil laws produce civil effects, which Christians will be bound, if they be just, to respect; if otherwise, might be compelled so to do; but they can never affect the matrimonial contract amongst Christians, it being the same matrimonial contract wnich was raised by our Lord to the dignity of Sacrament—not to be touched by profane hands, but exclusively confided to the church and its ministers. This is so clear that Calvin himself admits it, saying (Justit. Book 4th, chap. 19, § 37) : "Once admitted that Matrimony is a Sacrament, the matrimonial causes belong to them (the Pastors of the church), because spiritual things cannot be judged by the profane judges."

The church respects the civil laws, and even enforces them, whenever they are not in opposition to those of God and of her own ; but in case of any opposition between the laws of the church and those of the prince, or of the State, those of the church would stand, as to the validity or invalidity of the marriage contract before God, whatever might be the opinion and judgment of

men to the contrary, according to the words of our
Lord: "Whatsoever you shall bind upon earth, it shall
be bound also in heaven ; and whatsoever you shall
loose upon earth, it shall be loosed also in heaven"
(Matt. c. 18, v. 18), which particularly stands good for
what regards the Sacrament, as Matrimony is amongst
Christians.

The practice of the church in this respect confirms
the same truth ; for she, invariably, from the time of the
Apostles down to the present day, in all her tribunals,
judged upon the validity or invalidity of the matrimonial
tie, even amongst princes and kings, according as they
were contracted in conformity with her own laws, or
against them, without any regard to the civil laws of the
country in which they had been contracted. Therefore she constantly held this doctrine, that the civil laws
cannot affect the matrimonial contract amongst Christians, this being exclusively confided to the Divine founder, and she, most strenuously sustained the trust committed to her, in preserving inviolate the sanctity of
matrimony, its unity and indissolubility, according to
God's institution, against all the efforts even of crowned
heads who attempted to assail them ; opposing to their
mighty will and threats, her patience, constancy, and
perseverance, in telling them, in the name of the Lord,
as Saint John the Baptist to Herod, *non licet*, "it is not
lawful" (Mark c. 6, v. 18). The church, moreover,
has surrounded the Christian marriage with many wise
laws, which Christians cannot lawfully disregard ; but
are to observe them most carefully, if they wish to find
in the matrimonial state, not a source of anguish and
despair, but the happy fruits of domestic peace. Thanks

then to the untiring zeal of the church, or rather, to our
Lord, who has intrusted to his faithful spouse the interests of Christian marriage, and withdrawn it from profane hands, thus preserving the same, as Saint Paul
wished it to be, "honorable in all things." (Heb. c. 13,
v. 4.)

The church of God ever faithful to God's commis-
sion, to "preach the Gospel to every creature," and to
"teach all nations" the Gospel truths (Mark, c. 16, v.
15, and Matt. c. 28, v. 19), never ceased to inculcate
the unity and indissolubility of marriage as established
by God for all men, wherever she has announced the
tidings of salvation ; and she never allowed any devia-
tion from it, unless authorized by the same author of
matrimony and specified in the Gospel. She enacts no
laws of her own for them that are out of her pale, following in this the example of Saint Paul, who, writing
to the Corinthians (1st Cor. c. 5, vv. 12, 13) says :—
"What have I to do to judge them that are without?
. . . For they that are without God will judge." But
she did not neglect the Christian marriage ; and her
legislation in this respect is the most perfect code of
laws that ever existed, full of wisdom from above, because it is grounded on the Gospel. And first of all,
well aware of the prohibition of Polygamy, or plurality
of wives, made by Jesus Christ under the Christian dispensation, as we have seen before, she hath declared it
an article of Divine faith, and condemned as heretics
such as would dare to deny it, or affirm that it is lawful for Christians to have several wives simultaneously
(Can. 2, Sec. 24) : "If any one say that it is lawful
for Christians to have several wives simultaneously, and

that the Divine law prohibits the same, let him be anathema." The law of the church, contained in this definition, plainly embraces all Christians; but that the law of God, on which the same is grounded, extends to all men, whether Jews or Gentiles, or any other kind of Mormons, is also evinced by the practice of the same church; for in case of the conversion of any of them to the Catholic church who, whilst in their infidelity, had attempted to contract matrimony with several women, she does not allow them to keep but one of them, and that must be the first, as she is considered the only proper wife. Only in the event that the first wife would not live peaceably with the new convert, or would withdraw from him, in such case he would be allowed to leave the first, and take any one of the others unto wife, according to the liberty which the Gospel grants, in favor of the Christian faith, to the new convert. And this is the doctrine of the great Apostle, saying (1st Cor. c. 7, v. 15): "If the unbeliever depart, let him depart; for a brother or sister is not under bondage in such cases; but God hath called us in peace."

We need not repeat what we have said concerning the indissolubility of the marriage contract as established by God from the beginning, since the same was confirmed by our Lord Jesus Christ, and raised to the dignity of a Sacrament, under the new Dispensation; the same doctrine, therefore, is to be applied to Matrimony as a Sacrament; and the church grounded on said Divine teachings, and also on that of the Apostle: "To them that are married not I, but the Lord commandeth that the wife depart not from her husband; and if she depart that she remain unmarried, or be reconciled to her husband. And let not the husband put away his wife." And again : " A woman is bound by the law as long as her husband liveth; but if her husband die, she is at liberty ; let her marry whom she will, only in the Lord " (1st Cor. c. 7, vv. 10, 11, 39). And again : " The woman that hath a husband, whilst her husband liveth is bound to the law ; but if her husband be dead, she is loosed from the law of her husband. Wherefore, whilst her husband liveth, she shall be called an adulteress, if she be with another man " (Rom. c. 7, v. 2, 3). Grounded, I say, on these eternal truths, in which only death is assigned for the dissolution of the matrimonial tie amongst Christians, the church hath justly declared matrimony indissoluble, only by the death of one of the parties ; and declared heretics such as would dare affirm that it can be dissolved, either by heresy or troublesome cohabitation, or by a protracted absence of one of the parties, saying : " If any one say that the tie of matrimony can be dissolved either by heresy or troublesome cohabitation, or by a protracted absence of one of the parties, let him be anathema " (Can. 5, Sec. 24). She hath, moreover, condemned as heretics, and pronounced the same anathema against those who dare say that " the church errs, teaching that according to the evangelical and apostolic doctrine, that the band of matrimony cannot be dissolved for the cause of fornication of either of the married couple ; and that neither of the two—even the innocent, who did not give any cause for the adultery, cannot contract another martrimony whilst the other party lives ; but rather, that both, he who puts away the adulteress and marries another committeth adultery, and she who puts away the adulterer and is

2

married to another, committeth adultery." (Can. 7, Sec. 23.)

This doctrine of the church, which is that of the Apostle, as we have seen, and is derived from that of Jesus Christ, " What, therefore, God hath joined together, let no man put asunder," evidently is applicable to all men, since Jesus Christ legislates for mankind, as we have established before ; and therefore the church hath never, nor shall she ever recognize the validity of a matrimony contracted in virtue of a divorce from a previous marriage validly contracted. She rather looks always upon it as an adulterous union, according to that of our Lord, " Whosoever shall put away his wife and marry another, committeth adultery against her ; and if the wife shall put away her husband and be married to another, she committeth adultery." (Mark, c. 10, vv. 11, 12.) Nor can any Christian at any time, under any pretext whatever, apply to any civil magistrate or any court whatever for a divorce of a marriage validly contracted for the purpose of marrying another, or avail himself of a divorce previously obtained to get married again to another. The only exception that exists in this respect is the one mentioned above by Saint Paul, in favor of the Christian faith, when marriage has been contracted by two infidels, or unbaptized persons, and one of them after marriage embraces the Christian faith ; if the unbeliever abandons him, or will not live peaceably with the new convert, this remains free from the first tie, and can get married to another : " If the unbeliever depart, let him depart ; for a brother or sister is not under bondage in such cases ; but God has called us in peace." The reasonableness of this allowance appears plain from the very fact that it would be a great obstacle to embracing the Christian faith, without which " it is impossible to please God" (Heb. c. 11, v. 6), if the new convert were bound either to remain with an enemy or persecutor of his faith, or remain forever unmarried ; and therefore, when such is not the case, the tie of marriage continues good, and the new convert is bound to keep the infidel or unbaptized companion, according to the teaching of the same Apostle, saying, "If any brother have a wife that believeth not, and she consent to dwell with him, let him not put her away ; and if any woman have a husband that believeth not, and he consent to dwell with her, let her not put away her husband." (1st Cor. c. 7, vv. 12, 13.) As the above liberty and exception is only in favor of the Christian faith, it follows that a catholic, who, with dispensation from the church, would get married to an infidel or unbaptized person, could not avail himself of it to put away his companion and get married to another, although ill-treated and persecuted on account of his faith; but must of necessity abide by its consequences (which he well knows, or at least he should know) until the death of either of them.

This is the doctrine of the catholic church concerning the unity and perpetuity of the Christian marriage under the new dispensation ; and since it is in accordance with the teachings of the gospel, as we have observed, it is to be expected that no learned and reasonable man, comparing the same with the teaching of the politicians of this day and the practice of the church with that of civil courts, which are so generous in granting, for very trivial causes, divorces ; and, particularly, comparing

the effects produced by holding strictly to the severity
of the church with the looseness of morals caused by
deviating from the same—no reasonable man can re-
proach the first to praise the latter; but rather will
admire the divine wisdom by which the church has
always been guided, and will deeply lament the evils
brought on the domestic family by the Reformation,
depriving the Christian matrimony, under the pretext
of Christian liberty, of its sacred character as a sacrament, to withdraw the same from the pontiff and give it
to the king. In vain did the Reformers repent afterwards, and would reclaim the right of the church and
its pontiff for themselves; the evil seed was sown, and
it must produce its bad fruit. But the right of the
church is always the same; the matrimonial contract is
a sacrament; is one and indissoluble; its administration
is confided to the pastors of the church, who alone, of
their own authority, can establish laws regulating the
same and affecting its validity and lawfulness, which all
Christians are bound to observe, as we have heretofore
proved. We have, moreover, seen the doctrine of the
church concerning the unity and perpetuity of the
Christian marriage, and her laws protecting the same.
It remains now for us to consider, in particular, the
laws of the church affecting the Christian marriage,
both as a contract and as a sacrament, and which are
called impediments; as also those which do not affect
indeed the Christian marriage, but merely prescribe
some things to be observed in order to proceed cau-
tiously and prudently in an engagement which lasts for
life, and on which depend both the happiness of the
contracting parties and the fruits of domestic peace, and
greatly contribute to the good of society at large.

The laws of the church prohibiting marriage between certain persons are those which we call impediments; and they either render the contract null and void, or without annulling the contract, they render it only unlawful unless dispensed with by the same church. We have already proved that the church can establish such impediments, and therefore she can also dispense with the same, since every power authorized to make laws is equally empowered either to annul or dispense with the same, or to change them, according as the circumstances and good of the persons concerned may require; the power being given, as Saint Paul says (2d Cor. c. 10, v. 8), " for edification, and not for destruction." The church cannot, however, dispense with such impediments as are not established by herself, but by nature or the natural law ; hence she cannot allow those persons to contract matrimony whom the nature of the matrimonial contract itself repels, whether it be for want of understanding to know the nature of the engagement as incapable to contract, or for want of capacity to consummate the matrimonial tie as unfit for generation—such persons are said to labor under natural impediments to contract matrimony, nor can they be dispensed by any authority whatever; neither can the church dispense with the laws of God prohibiting marriage, under the Christian dispensation, to them that are already validly engaged in this state until one of the parties die, as we have seen, speaking of the unity and indissolubility of matrimony, and which the divines call an impediment of divine institution. She can, however, dispense with those impediments, or laws prohibiting marriage, within certain degrees of kindred, which God gave to his people, and are contained in the 18th chapter of the Book of Leviticus ; both because they do not regard Christians, having been abrogated by the gospel, nor are they imposed by the natural law, which alone is obligatory at all times and to all persons ; and hence the church hath justly pronounced, in the Council of Trent, the following anathema : " If any one say that only those degrees of consanguinity and affinity which are mentioned in the Book of Leviticus can prohibit matrimony and annul its contract, nor can the church dispense with some of them, or establish that some others may prohibit or annul the same, let him be anathema." (Can. 3, Sess. 24.)

We are therefore reduced to the laws of the church prohibiting marriage, rendering it either null and void if attempted, or at least unlawful if contracted without her dispensation. Hence there are two kinds of ecclesiastical impediments, namely, those that both prohibit the matrimonial contract and annul it if attempted, and those that merely prohibit it, but if contracted, although unlawfully, yet becomes binding and obligatory in conscience. The knowledge of them being of the highest importance to the persons called to the matrimonial state, and showing likewise the wisdom of the church on this most interesting subject, we cannot forbear mentioning them. They are contained in the following verses :

" Error, conditio, votum, cognatio, crimen,
" Cultus disparitas, vis, ordo ligamen, honestas,
" Amens, affinis, si clandestinus, et impos,
" Si mulier sit rapta loco nec reddita tuto."

These forbid marriage, and annul it if attempted.

The following merely forbid it, but it is valid if contracted ; they are :

"Ecclesæ vetitum, tempus, sponsalia, votum."

We cannot be expected, however, to give a full
explanation of these impediments, which would be a
tedious work, would require a volume, and would answer little to our purpose ; it being only to show the
wisdom of the church in her legislation, and to caution the faithful how they ought to proceed prudently,
and always with advice from their pastors, in matrimonial concerns.

We commence with those impediments which annul
the matrimonial contract, the first and eleventh of which
—namely, Error and Insanity, " *Error et Amens* "—
are natural impediments for want of consent ; the ninth,
" *Ligamen*," that is, the tie of matrimony previously
contracted, still existing, of divine enactment ; the
eighth and fourteenth, " *Vis et Iinpos*," force and violence and impotency are partly natural and partly ecclesiastical ; the fifth, tenth, and thirteenth are purely
ecclesiastical, such are Crime, Honesty, and Clandestinity, " *crimen, honestas, clandestinus ;*" and the second,
third, fourth, sixth, eighth, twelfth, and fifteenth, are
also indeed ecclesiastical, but most conformable to the
natural or divine law—that is to say, to reason and revelation ; such are Condition, Vow, Kindred, " *conditio,
votum, cognatio*," Disparity of worship, Order, Affinity,
"*cultus disparitas, ordo affinis ;*" and finally, Rape, " *si
mulier sit rapta*," etc.

The first impediment is Error, and exists whenever
any individual marries a person intending to marry another ; the matrimony is null for want of consent.

The second is Condition, which means the state or condition of slavery, and annuls matrimony when a free person marries a slave not knowing such to be bond. The church annuls this matrimony, as a free and full consent cannot be supposed, such as matrimony requires. Hence if the condition of slavery be known by the free party, the matrimony is valid and good; since nature has given to every one the right to select the companion for life, whether free or bond, unless prohibited by proper authority and for good reasons, which the church cannot see in this case.

The third is a Vow; that is to say, a solemn and perpetual vow made in a religious community approved by the church. By such vow a person binds himself to live in perpetual celibacy, in order to be more " solicitous," as St. Paul says (1st Cor. c. 7, v. 32), "for the things that belong to the Lord, how he may please God." As such vow is pleasing to God, and of the highest importance for the persons that make it to be faithful to the engagement, the church, both to prevent rashness and precipitation in making it, and to facilitate its observance after being made, has declared a matrimony contracted after that, unless it be dispensed with, null and void.

The fourth is Kindred, or Consanguinity. The canon law distinguishes three different kinds of relationship or kindred : the first proceeding from the communication of blood, which is called consanguinity ; the second, from the office of godfather or godmother in baptism and confirmation, and this is called spiritual kindred ; and the third from the perfect adoption of some one as a son or daughter, with the right of inheritance,

which last is known by the name of legal kindred. The
first, or consanguinity, annuls matrimony between persons related within the fourth degree of kindred, computing the degrees with the generations. The reasons
which the church has in establishing this impediment are
the same which God had in prohibiting marriage to the
Jews within certain degrees (Leviticus, c. 18) ; such as,
for example, to diffuse the bonds of amity, friendship,
and relationship amongst strange families, uniting them
in charity ; to inspire respect and avoid unlawful familiarity amongst kindred, entertaining no hope of marriage amongst them ; the perfecting of the human race,
both in its corporeal and mental faculties, to which the
mixture of blood greatly contributes, whilst the contrary
practice gradually enervates them. (This, young people who intend to marry, should bear in mind.) Here
we may observe what divines affirm, that kindred in
direct line hinders matrimony in any degree whatever ;
and even nature abhors it, at least in the first degree,
both direct and collateral line ; and hence they say that
within said degree it is a natural impediment, in which
therefore the church has never dispensed.

The spiritual kindred, resulting from baptism and
confirmation, is an impediment established by the
church, and annuls matrimony between the godfather
or godmother and the godchild ; and between the same
godfather or godmother and the father or mother of the
godchild. The godfathers taking the place of parents
with respect to their godchildren, in the spiritual order,
to instruct them in the things concerning their salvation,
most wisely the church has established the impediment
to prevent all dangers of temptation in the fulfillment of

2*

their duty, removing from them the hope of a future matrimony. The same impediment exists between the person that administers baptism or confirmation and the person baptized or confirmed and their parents, as the spiritual kindred extends also to them.

For the same reasons above stated, the church has also established the impediment of legal kindred, and annuls the matrimony, in direct line, between the adopter and adopted and the children of the adopted to the fourth generation; in the collateral line, between the adopted and the children of the adopter only whilst the adoption perseveres; and by affinity, between the adopter and the wife of the adopted, and, *vice versa*, between the wife of the adopter and the adopted.

The fifth impediment is Crime ; namely, the crime of murder, of adultery, and of both murder and adultery, annul matrimony in the following cases : The crime of murdering the wife or the husband being agreed upon with a third person, with the intention of marrying afterwards, annuls the projected matrimony if the murder be committed; the crime of adultery committed with a promise of marriage after the death of the husband, or of the wife of either of the parties, annuls also the promised matrimony, when both the adultery and promise have occurred during the same first marriage ; likewise a second matrimony contracted during the life of one's husband or wife, not only is null, but it renders the persons who attempted the marriage unfit to marry even after the death of the first companion, provided that both knew the first husband or wife to be still alive. Finally, the two crimes of murder and adultery occur when either the adulterer murders the husband of the

adulteress, or the adulteress kills the wife of the adul·
terer, with the intention of contracting matrimony afterwards ; they cannot marry, and if they attempt it, their
matrimony is null and void. The wisdom of the church
establishing this impediment is evident, the object being
to protect fidelity amongst married people and prevent
crime.

The sixth impediment, Disparity of Worship, is that
which annuls matrimony between two persons, the one
baptized and the other unbaptized, already forbidden by
the Apostle, saying, " Bear not the yoke together with
unbelievers " (2d Cor. c. 6, v. 14), of which we shall
have occasion to speak afterwards.

The seventh is Force or Violence, which if it be such
as to deprive a person altogether of liberty, is a natural
impediment ; but it is an ecclesiastical impediment when
it is such as to affect a person with a grievous fear,
caused by a free agent, unjustly, in order to obtain the
consent ; this annuls matrimony, as an onerous contract
of such importance demands freedom and full consent ;
for the protection of which the church established said
impediment ; and, moreover, she forbids all persons,
even masters and magistrates, whether directly or indi-
rectly, to force in any way their subjects to contract
matrimony, under the pain of excommunication, which
they incur by the very fact. (Council of Trent, Sess.
24, Chap. 9.)

The eighth is Order ; namely, the Sacred Order, by
which a Levite consecrates himself irrevocably to the
service of the ministry, as we said of the vow, to be
more free to attend to the things of God.

The ninth is " Ligamen," a previous matrimony validly contracted. As we have said, this is of divine institution, the tie being perpetual.

The tenth, Public Honesty. This has been established by the church for the reasons conveyed by the very name, and already explained, speaking of consanguinity; and springs from two sources, namely, from espousals or a lawful contract of a future matrimony, and from matrimony contracted but not consummated. The first annuls the matrimony contracted by one of the sponsors with the relatives of the other within the first degree of consanguinity, that is to say, with the father or mother, and with the brother or sister; and the second annuls the same within the fourth degree, even should the first matrimony contracted and not consummated be null, with the only exception that such nullity were for want of consent.

The eleventh is Insanity. Nature renders insane persons incapable to contract, except they had intervals of reason, during which they could contract matrimony —this being not prohibited by the church.

The twelfth, Affinity; which is the kindred resulting from the mutual intercourse of both sexes, each of whom contracts affinity with the relatives, by blood or consanguinity, of the other. The said intercourse may be lawful when in lawful marriage, or unlawful; in the first case it annuls matrimony within the fourth degree, and in the second within the second only, computing the degrees of affinity by those of consanguinity. By mutual intercourse, although unlawful, man and woman are made one flesh, according to the doctrine of Saint Paul, " He who adheres to a harlot is made one body." (1st Cor. c. 6, v. 16.) Hence the degree of consanguinity on one side forms the degree of affinity on the other. This impediment, within certain degrees, was established by God himself for the Jews (Leviticus, c. 18) ; but, as we observed before, such is no more binding to Christians; therefore the impediment is ecclesiastical, the same reasons guiding the church in establishing it which God had of old for his people.

The thirteenth impediment is Clandestinity, of which we shall have occasion to speak afterwards ; and therefore, it will be sufficient for the present to declare in what it consists, quoting the words of the Council of Trent, by which the said impediment is established, and which is of obligation wheresoever the same has been published, as is the case in California: " Whosoever will attempt to contract matrimony otherwise than in presence of the proper pastor, or some other priest authorized by the said pastor, or by the ordinary and two or three witnesses, such the Holy Synod renders wholly incapable of contracting, and declares such contracts null and void, as by the present decree annuls and declares them void." (Chap. 1, Sess. 24.) This impediment was most wisely established by the Church to protect the sanctity of the matrimonial contract, and prevent the awful evils that proceed from rash, precipitate, unpremeditated and secret engagements.

The fourteenth impediment is that of Impotency, which we said to be partly natural, partly ecclesiastical. Perpetual and absolute impotency, or incapacity of consummating matrimony is a natural impediment to the marriage state ; relative impotency is likewise a natural impediment, but only with regard to the persons in whose respect such impotency exists. Children, also, before the age of puberty, which for males is the age of fourteen years, and for females that of twelve, are incapable of contracting matrimony, according to the canon law; as they are considered incapable to consummate matrimony.

The fifteenth and last of the impediments that annul matrimony, is Rape, by which we mean the violent or forcible withdrawal of a woman from place to place, under the power of the raptor, for the purpose of contracting marriage; whilst the woman will be under the control and power of the raptor, although she might willingly consent, they cannot contract matrimony; and if they do, the contract will be null and void, the Church annulling the same for the purpose of securing the liberty of the engagement. To contract validly it is necessary that the woman be removed from the place and out of the power of the raptor, and set at liberty.

The impediments which do not annul the contract of matrimony, but render it unlawful, are, as we said before, four, namely: "Ecclesiæ vetitum, Tempus, Spousalia, Votum." The Prohibition of the Church, Time, Spousals, and Vow.

The Church may prohibit, for several reasons, the contracting of matrimony for a while; as she does sometimes for the purpose of ascertaining whether there be any impediment to it or not; and also to comply with certain requirements of the same Church, that the contracting parties may prepare themselves to receive worthily the sacrament and the fruits thereof. To contract, therefore, while her prohibition stands, is sinful and unlawful, although the contract will stand. This will be more fully understood in the sequel, as also why, on

certain times she prohibits some of the rites and ceremonies of the christian marriage, as unsuitable to the
spirit of the Church under certain circumstances.

Espousals, or the promise of a future matrimony, is
an obstacle or impediment to contract matrimony with
any other besides the one to whom the promise was
made, as it would be a violation or a breach of faith,
and therefore unlawful, unless the first promise were
null or mutually dissolved, or else, not binding for want
of fidelity or otherwise, in the person to whom the
promise was made. However, matrimony would be
valid and obligatory if contracted, notwithstanding such
promise, except in case it was contracted with a person
in the first degree of consanguinity to the person to
whom the promise had been made, as we said before.

Finally, the simple vow of Chastity, or of Celibacy,
or of entering a religious life ; and even the vow which
is made in such religious communities, who make simple
vows, not solemn, which, as we have said before, annul
matrimony. Such simple vows render matrimony unlawful, unless dispensed with ; but if it were contracted,
the matrimony would be valid and good.

Such are the laws of the Church affecting christian
marriage, and rendering it either null and void, or at
least unlawful ; for which reason they are justly called
Impediments. The Church enacting these laws, does
not intend to legislate for those that are out of her pale,
as we said before, according to the doctrine of Saint
Paul ; but for her children. Nevertheless, her laws
bind also, those who, although they may belong to other
denominations, have received christian baptism ; since
by baptism, when validly administered to them, they

become subjects of Jesus Christ, and debtors to him of the whole law; and consequently they were by him placed under the guidance of them to whom Christ confided his authority, saying: "As the Father hath sent me, I also send you;" * * "go, and teach all nations; baptising them, * * teaching them to observe all things whatsoever I have commanded you," and "whatsoever you shall bind upon earth, shall be bound also in heaven." (John, c. 20, v. 21; Matt. c. 28, vv. 10, 20; Matt. c. 18, v. 18.) The Church, however, does not intend to oblige them in several things, especially with regard to the marriage contract, in order to prevent its invalidity, and thus lessen the number of sins, and of even material transgressions of her laws; but they cannot avoid being bound by the laws of the Church whenever they are willing to contract marriage with a Catholic, it being impossible for the law to affect one party without affecting the other. The Church would prefer not to have anything to do with them, and let them alone, according to the doctrine of the Apostle: "what have I to do with them that are without?" and therefore she forbids Catholics to intermarry with them, as it was of old forbidden to the Jews to intermarry with the Gentiles. But according to the power which she hath received from God, she may allow such marriages, under certain conditions to remove the dangers which accompany them, and she does really allow them whenever the present state of society, or mixed up population seems to require it; as it is now in this our country, and generally throughout the United States; but always under certain conditions and her previous dispensation, without which a Catholic would sin mortally by marrying any one else but a Catholic; and the matrimony even, would be null and void, if contracted with an unbaptized person; or if baptized, with some of those impediments above mentioned, which the Church has declared to annul the matrimonial contract.

The Church forbidding Catholics to intermarry with any but Catholics, follows the doctrine of the Apostles, which no doubt, they learned from our Lord himself. If question be of unbaptized persons, we have the prohibition of Saint Paul, who writing to the Corinthians, speaking of marriage, says: " Bear not the yoke together with unbelievers; for what participation hath justice with injustice? or what fellowship hath light with darkness? and what concord hath Christ with Belial? or what part hath the faithful with the unbeliever?" (2d Ep. c. 6, vv. 14, 15.) And if of baptized persons, but that abandoned the ancient faith, and did not continue in the doctrine of Christ, the bloved disciple of our Lord says (2d Ep. c. —, vv. 10, 11) : "If any man come to you, and bring not this doctrine, receive him not into the house, nor say to him, God save you; for he that saith to him God save you, communicateth with his wicked works." Far be from us the blasphemous thought that the Apostle of Charity, whom Jesus loved, forbids by divine inspiration, the charitable intercourse and friendly dealings which we owe to all men; but he merely admonishes the faithful in general of the dangers which may arise from a familiarity with those who have gone from the true faith, whose speech, as Saint Paul says: "spreadeth like a cancer" (2d Tim. c. 2, v. 17), lest they might subvert "the faith of some." (Same 18.) Although this could not be applied, consistently with charity, to every case in particular; as on the contrary, there are many honest, generous, unprejudiced, and liberal minds amongst them that are out of Catholicity; and even not a few who are better than the Catholics themselves, as we are obliged, to our shame, to confess; as also did Saint Paul when complaining of a sin amongst the faithful Corinthians, unheard of even "among the Gentiles." (1st Ep. c. 5, v. 1.) Still, this cannot altogether destroy the dangers which the beloved disciple foresaw, and which unhappily too often result from said familiarity; which, therefore, the Church reasonably apprehends, and justify her in forbidding such marriages, unless contracted under certain conditions, to protect the faith of the Catholic party, and that of her offspring. Is it not just that the Church should protect the faith of her children? And would she not cease to be the true spouse of Jesus Christ, if she neglected the care and solicitude of her flock?

The conditions, then, prescribed by the Church, besides the dispensation of her law prohibiting such alliances, are to the effect of securing, first, "the free exercise of the Catholic religion to the Catholic party;" and secondly, "the Catholic education of the children of such marriages, both male and female." The first of these conditions is eminently just, by what we have already said concerning the care and solicitude that the Church must have as a tender mother, for the welfare and eternal salvation of her children, and the preservation of their faith, without which, as Saint Paul says: "It is impossible to please God:" Heb. c. 11, v. 6.) The second is not less evidently just, since the very nature of matrimony, as an institution of God, imperatively demands, if there be children, that they be raised in the knowledge and fear of God; and consequently educated in the true religion of the Crucified; and such does the Catholic Church know, as certain as God cannot lie, that she is. The very least, then, that the Church can require from the non-Catholic party, is a formal and solemn promise to that effect, without which she has never, and we dare say, she shall never, nor can she ever dispense. Nor can any Catholic, therefore, at any time, or under any circumstances whatever, contract such marriage with a person not Catholic, regardless of the above said dispensation and promise, without a grievous crime of disobedience to the Church, and exposing himself rashly to the danger, both of losing his faith and that of his children, and incurring the anathemas of the Church, it being in several dioceses prohibited under pain of excommunication, (as in the Diocese of Monterey and Los Angeles) : especially if said marriage were contracted before any minister of religion of any other denomination but Catholic, which is most severely forbidden by the Church; and in some dioceses (as in the above said, of Monterey and Los Angeles) excommunication is incurred by the very fact. The matrimony, however, would be binding and obligatory, except the case in which the party not Catholic were unbaptized; or if baptized, there existed between them any of those impediments above mentioned, which the Church has declared to render matrimony null and void, as we observed before.

According to the above said doctrine, it appears evident, that it is of the highest importance for the contracting parties, especially for the Catholic ones, before engaging in such marriages, in order not to expose themselves to the danger of disappointment, to apply in time to the Church for dispensation and direction; that all things being done in order, they may draw upon themselves God's blessing, of which they stand so much in need to discharge faithfully the arduous duties of the matrimonial state; for, what benefit could a Protestant, or any other not Catholic, expect from taking as his or her inseparable companion for life, a Catholic, who, regardless of the most sacred laws of the Church, would dare to trample under foot the institutions of his or her professed religion? What kind of affection, love, and respect, could he promise to himself, from one who thus disdains her God, her Church, and its Ministers, and even her own soul? Oh! unhappy Catholic who thus sneers at his God; for unless he repent and do penance for such sinful and foolish act, a day will come in which his despised Lord and Judge shall tell him in his turn, "you have despised all my counsel, and have neglected my reprehension; I also will laugh in your destruction." (Prov. c. 1, vv. 25, 26.)

We say, then, that for the Catholic party, especially, it is of the highest importance to proceed with prudence and caution before engaging in such mixed marriages, as his faith and perseverance is apt to be exposed to the severest trials, notwithstanding the dispensation of the church, and the promise of the other party not Catholic, to the effect of securing the free exercise of his religion and that of the children. This danger has often proved fatal to the soul; and as the same proceeds from the very nature of the matrimonial contract, whose tie is perpetual and indissoluble, for this reason the Catholic church has always abhorred and detested the said mixed marriages, and prohibited them, as we have shown, they being prejudicial to Christianity. And in fact, except the case in which the Catholic succeeds in converting his companion to the Catholic faith and its practice, which he is bound to procure, both by word and example, what will be the effects produced by these marriages with regard to the faith and morals of the Catholic party and children? We know that many a Catholic lady married to a Protestant or even Infidel gentleman (and *vice versa*), who are models of piety in the practice of their religion; whose husbands, rather than put any obstacle in their way, encourage them; affording them besides every facility to promote the Catholic education of their children, faithful to the promise they made when they were married. But even in this case, what will be the effects produced, both to the wife and children, by the zeal of the father, unsupported by example? Will he be able to persuade them of the necessity of the Catholic faith and its practice, he himself remaining outside of it? Can it be reasonably supposed that even his dearest ones will follow rather the way and the faith of the mother than that of their father? And if he were willing to insist, would they not be justified in saying to him: "Physician, heal thyself?" (Luke, c. 4, v. 24.) And should the pious mother succeed in raising her beloved children in the bosom of the Catholic church, shall she not suffer the anguish and pain of seeing some of them, when grown, following the example of their father, abandon the faith which they had embraced in their infancy? and thus perhaps introduce into the same family with the difference of belief and of religion that of discord and of infidelity? Oh! would to God, that the pious and virtuous mother may not see in her old age some of her dearest ones to sneer and laugh at her own faith and religion! The fact is, that from such mixed marriages, even the most fortunate ones, proceed infidel children; neither Catholics nor Protestants; loving no religion at all, if not hating every religion. If such be the case in these marriages, contracted even under the best auspices, what must be the unhappy lot of a Catholic marrying one, who, faithless to the promise made, as not seldom is the case, becomes, not so much his opponent, as his tyrant and persecutor on account of his faith, unless he have the virtue of a Saint to suffer a protracted martyrdom!

We may be told, that to the same dangers might be exposed a Catholic marrying another Catholic. It is true, if question be of a Catholic who lost his faith—an impious Catholic, who is still worse than an infidel; and therefore what we said above is equally applicable to the case. Since we speak of the dangers and trials to which the faith of the Catholic party and that of the children may be exposed—for want of faith and discrepancy of religion in the married couple—besides which, there are other dangers resulting from the want of good morals, in either of the contracting parties, which may be equally found in a Protestant and in a Catholic—as well in a non-professing Catholic as in an Infidel—whether baptized or unbaptized. This increases the necessity of being on the alert, when question is of making selection of a companion for life, and not to be led by impetuous passion, but by reason and faith.

In these mixed marriages the church dispenses with

all the sacred ceremonial rites, not only for the sake of
the non-Catholic party, from whom she does not wish to
force any external act contrary to conscientious convic-
tions ; but also in behalf of the Catholic party, she wishes
to have the same contracted under her protection, represented by the Catholic Priest. She forbids even the
Clergyman to perform any sacred rite in these marriages, both in order not to appear to approve them—
for she rather tolerates than approves them, for the reasons above said ; and also in order not to coöperate
in any way to the profanation of the Sacrament, in case
that the not Catholic party be not well disposed, as it
is justly supposed, to receive the grace of the same ;
whether for want of good faith in his religious belief, or
for want of conviction that Matrimony under the Christian Dispensation is one of the seven sacraments established by our Lord Jesus Christ. We may be asked,
is then Matrimony a sacrament, when contracted between a Catholic and non-Catholic? We must answer
with distinction ; either the non-Catholic party has been
baptized or not ; certainly it cannot be a sacrament for
the non-Catholic, if he has not been baptized ; as baptism is the door by which one enters into the sanc-
tuary of the church, becomes a member of the mys-
tical body of our Lord, and a child of God ; and as
such he is made partaker of the pastures which Jesus
Christ left for his children in the sacrament, in which
he cannot partake who is unbaptized ; but if the non-
Catholic party be validly baptized, whosoever he may
be that administered it, and in whatsoever denomination
of Christians he may have received the same, as there
is but "one Lord, one faith, one baptism, one God and

the Father of all " (Eph. c. 4, vv. 5, 6); moreover, whether it be Peter or Paul, John or Judas, who administers Christian baptism ; even more, whether it be a male or a female who performs this rite, it is the same as to its validity, because it is Christ himself who baptizes, " He it is that baptizeth with the Holy Ghost," says Saint John (c. 1, v. 33) ; therefore, such a one by baptism became a member of the Christian family, and consequently capable to receive all the sacraments of the church, as to their validity—matrimony included. Still something else is required on their part to receive the sacraments, when they attain to the use of reason, which is the intention of receiving them. If said intention be not wanting, certainly they receive the sacrament of matrimony ; but if they do not intend to receive the sacrament of matrimony, whether it be because they do not believe it to be a sacrament, or for some other reason. In such case theologians are divided, some saying that they do not receive the sacrament ; but others, even more probably think, that they always receive the sacrament, whether they intend or not, provided both be baptized, and intend seriously to perform the matrimonial contract, since this very contract, as we said above, was raised by our Lord unto the dignity of a sacrament amongst Christians ; and consequently, the sacrament being inseparable from the matrimonial contract, whenever this matrimonial contract is validly performed, there is also the Sacrament of Matrimony amongst baptized persons.

As for the Catholic party, in these mixed marriages, Divines incline in favor of considering it always a sacrament, at least, when both parties have been baptized;

and hence the Catholic is bound to prepare himself to receive the grace, which is annexed to the sacrament, and which it never fails to produce, when received with proper dispositions. What is the preparation required from a Catholic, or what dispositions must he have not merely not to profane the sacrament, but also to receive its fruits, we proceed now to examine — referring to the laws of the church regulating the Christian marriage, when contracted by two Catholics.

These laws either command something previous to the matrimonial engagement or accompanying the same, or even subsequent to it. In other words, the church commands some things to be observed before marriage, others in the time of marriage, and some others after the marriage is contracted. The first are intended by way of preparation ; the second of consecration ; and the last perfection ; and they teach the contracting parties how they are to prepare themselves to receive the grace of the sacrament ; that they are to receive it with the utmost reverence and devotion ; and finally, that they have to endeavor to preserve the fruits thereof. Before marriage the church commands the bans of matrimony to be published three successive Sundays or festival days in the parochial church, of those that intend to be married ; entreating them meanwhile to prepare themselves, by approaching the holy sacraments of Penance and Holy Eucharist. In the time of marriage she commands the contracting parties to contract the same in the presence of the proper Pastor, or of another Priest, authorized by said Pastor, or the Bishop, who is to confirm their contract, and sanctify it, by imploring upon them, and granting to them God's holy benediction.

3

And, finally, after matrimony has been contracted, she anxiously wishes to implore for them, at the most Holy Sacrifice of the Mass, all those temporal and spiritual blessings, of which they stand so much in need, to comply faithfully with the duties of the married state, and that they may find therein the happy fruits of domestic peace and everlasting enjoyment; and therefore she imposes on them the duty on certain days and occasions to assist, after the ceremony of matrimony, at the Holy Sacrifice of the Mass for the performance of this rite.

In the first place, the church commands the bans of matrimony to be published before marriage can be contracted; and this she does for very wise and weighty reasons. First, to discover whether there be any impediment to the proposed marriage; and secondly, to obtain God's grace in behalf of the couple to be married through the prayers of the Congregation. It is of the highest importance to the contracting parties to know and discover whether there be or not any impediment to the intended marriage which would render it null and void, and a mere palliated concubinage; and as there might be some, which it is impossible for them to know, on account of its secrecy, unless discovered by others, so the church by this means takes the most efficacious step to secure the interested parties in this respect, commanding, under pain of mortal sin and even excommunication, all and every Catholic who may know any of these impediments (except such as may be known only under natural secrecy, or by reason of professional duties, which are not subject to denunciation), to discover them to the Pastor, that proper means may be taken either to stop the marriage or to obtain beforehand the proper dispensation. Thus the church, as a solicitous Mother, secures the honor of the contracting parties and that of their families, as well as that of the matrimonial engagement, which is called by Saint Paul "honorable" (Heb. c. 13, v. 4). By this any one can easily perceive how great folly it is for the contracting parties to present objections to the observance of this wise law of the church, which places them on secure ground in making the most important of all contracts. Oh! how many an honorable young lady, by neglecting the said wise prescription, contrary to the will of her Pastor, from whom she forced a dispensation, often for no other reason than to avoid having her name mentioned in the church, has afterwards discovered with anguish, bitterness, and despair, that the object of her affection had given his previously to another! It is in order to prevent such calamities that the church recommends to her Pastors seldom to dispense with the matrimonial bans, and then only for just and very grievous reasons. If Catholics were to understand well their interests, rather than solicit any dispensation on this point, they would urge having said laws rigorously enforced in their regard; and this, not only to prevent disappointment, but even to obtain the prayers of the faithful. The other reason for which the church commands the bans of matrimony to be published:

Society at large is greatly interested in matrimonial contracts, but especially Christian society. All legislators have recognized, with the church, which has been commanded to civilize the world by the preaching of the gospel, that the well-being and harmony of a nation, or even of society, as we observed elsewhere, greatly depends on the well-regulated family, the result of matrimonial contract, as the collection of these small societies forms what we call a nation, or society; hence the zeal of the church in enacting laws to regulate the Christian marriage, as she is the only competent Legislator, who can fully comprehend God's holy requirements in this respect, the Christian marriage being, as we proved before, one of the seven sacraments of the new law, whose dispensation has been confided to her by our Lord. The church, therefore, well aware of the importance of matrimony for the good of society, and especially for that of Christian society, she not only prays but recommends all her children to pray for such as have been called to the marriage state, and are about engaging in it, that God may vouchsafe to direct all their proceedings to the greatest glory and the welfare of Christianity. It is for this same reason that the church entreats the contracting parties, whilst the bans of matrimony are being published, to prepare themselves for the reception of this sacrament, approaching worthily the holy sacraments of Penance and Holy Communion, that their souls being thus purified from the stain of mortal sin, and fortified with the Body and Blood of our Lord Jesus Christ, they may render themselves worthy of that supernatural love which will enable them to be mutually assiduous and diligent in complying with each other's wish, seeking each other's comfort, and bearing the mutual yoke with gladness and edification,—the proper fruits of the sacramental grace attached by our Lord, through the merits of his passion and death, to matrimony under the Christian dispensation.

Although the minister of the sacrament of matrimony

be not the priest, but the contracting parties themselves, according to the teaching of the Catholic church, which is an additional reason for them to receive before the sacraments of penance and holy eucharist, still the church has at all times enjoined upon the faithful the duty of receiving the sacrament of matrimony under the protection of the church, represented by her minister, the proper pastor of the contracting parties, who is to ratify the matrimonial contract, imploring and imparting unto them God's holy benediction ; and impelled by the weightiest reasons, she has enjoined this wherever the Council of Trent has been published, as it is in our State (California), not only under the pain of mortal sin, but she has even declared the matrimonial contract null and void whenever attempted in places where there is a parish priest resident, to whom they may have recourse conveniently. However, Catholics who live in places or counties remote from the church and far from the priest's residence, as for example those who reside in the interior of the State, or to whom it would be almost impossible, notwithstanding their good will, to have recourse to the priest and contract in his presence, in which the church does not invalidate their matrimonial contract, provided they contract before at least two witnesses, and if possible Catholics ; even in this case the Catholic church enjoins on them the duty, as soon as they will have the opportunity, to receive the priest's blessing and have the matrimonial contract ratified by the same. From this it appears evident, that those Catholics who, disregarding the laws of the church in this respect, dare to contract matrimony before the civil magistrates, or any other way, without the presence of the Catholic priest, in cities and places where the said priest resides or visits, besides committing a mortal sin, cause great scandal to religion and do great injury to themselves, living in a state of degradation, their matrimony being nothing else but a palliated concubinage, which will surely bring them to eternal condemnation, unless they repent and repair the scandal by redressing their steps; such the church wishes to have cut off from her communion by the sword of excommunication (Conc. Tri. Sess. 24, Cap. 8, De Reform.), and in the diocese of Monterey and Los Angeles they incur the same by the very fact.

After the ceremony of matrimony is performed, the church enjoins on them that have been married to assist at the holy sacrifice of the mass, and receive therein a still more copious benediction, the nuptial blessing. This is one of the most imposing ceremonies of the church, and one which Catholics should not disregard. It is only enjoined on them who are married for the first time, nor can it be performed at all times, the church prohibiting the performance of this rite from the first Sunday in Advent until the day of the Epiphany, and from Ash Wednesday to the octave of Easter, inclusively; on which time she recommends to her children not to contract matrimony at all, for reason of the penitential time and the great mysteries which are commemorated, and the faithful are expected to comply with their mother's wish in order not to be deprived of the above especial blessing, which, as we have said, is one of the most touching and imposing ceremonies of the Catholic church, and shows evidently the great respect and esteem in which Christian marriage is to

be held. The holy sacrifice of the mass is offered up
for the new couple, and the whole of the liturgy is
directed towards obtaining for them Heaven's most
copious blessings, commencing the Introit with those
words of Raguel when he gave Sara his daughter in
marriage to Tobias : " The God of Abraham, and the
God of Isaac, and the God of Jacob be with you, and
may He join you together and fulfil his blessing in
you " (Tob. c. 7, v. 15), and so on to the end of the
mass. Mindful of the divine institution of marriage,
of its being a great sacrament in Christ and in the
church, and of the duties resulting from it for the newly
married, she implores the grace that they may fulfill
them ; that being faithful to the Author of matrimony,
they may live a long life, and see their children's children to the third and fourth generation. She reads
that portion of the Epistle of St. Paul to the Ephesians
(chap. 5, from v. 22 to 33) in which he details the duties
of both husband and wife, and that they are to cherish
one another as Christ and his church, of whose union
matrimony is a figure ; and, particularly, that the husband " love his wife as himself," and " the wife reverence her husband." She reads also that portion of the
gospel (Matthew, c. 19, vv. 3–6) in which our Lord
declares matrimony to be instituted by God, one and
indissoluble. And in one of the most solemn moments
of the sacrifice, immediately after the " Paternoster" or
Lord's Prayer, she pronounces a lengthy benediction on
both the bridegroom and the bride, but most particularly
on the bride, begging of God that she may " be pleasing
to her husband, like Rachel ; discreet, like Rebecca ;
and in years and fidelity, like Sarah." Finally, at the

end of mass, before giving the last blessing, she addresseth likewise both of them, saying, "May the God of Abraham, the God of Isaac, and the God of Jacob be with you, and may He fulfil his blessing in you, that you may see your children's children to the third and fourth generation ; and afterwards enter the possession of eternal life, through the assistance of our Lord Jesus Christ, who, with the Father and the Holy Ghost, liveth and reigneth one God forever. Amen." Such are the laws and ceremonies prescribed by the church for Catholic marriages. Would to God they were faithfully observed by Christians ! There would not be so many unhappy marriages and scandals in Christian society.

Having considered matrimony under its two-fold aspect, as a contract and as a sacrament, under the Christian dispensation ; its essential qualities of unity, sanctity, and indissolubility ; the different erroneous doctrines opposed to the same as an institution of God ; the power and zeal of the Catholic church in protecting Christian marriage by prudent and wise laws, it seems to us that our object would remain yet imperfect unless we placed before the reader the duties resulting from Christian marriage, the knowledge of which may greatly contribute to direct those who feel themselves called to that state, how they ought to proceed with the utmost care, rectitude of intention, and guided by religion in embracing it. This is what we are going to do in the following lines :

The duties resulting from matrimony, called by Saint Paul a " Yoke " (2d Cor. c. 6, v. 14), are of such importance and so arduous that the disciples of our Lord hearing him speak of them, and especially of those resulting from its perpetuity, said to him, "If the case of a man with his wife be so, it is not good to marry;" that is to say, it is better not to marry. To whom the Lord, approving their opinion, said, "All receive not this word, but they to whom it is given" (Matt. c. 19, vv. 10, 11); and hence He took occasion to extol and enhance celibacy over the matrimonial state, saying: "There are eunuchs who have made themselves eunuchs for the kingdom of heaven's sake," and encouraged them to celibacy, adding, "He that can receive it, let him receive it." (Same, v. 12.) St. Paul also recommends celibacy and virginity over the matrimonial state, as being more apt to attend to the service of God and to one's salvation, saying, "He that is without a wife is solicitous for the things that belong to the Lord, how he may please God; but he that is with a wife is solicitous for the things of the world, how he may please his wife, and he is divided. And the unmarried woman and the virgin thinketh on the things of the Lord, that she may be holy both in body and spirit; but she that is married thinketh on the things of the world, how she may please her husband." (1st Cor. 7.) Concerning this, however, there is no commandment, except for such who freely, of their own choice, impose upon themselves the obligation and vow chastity and celibacy to the Lord, having received the gift from him; but it is only advised as more perfect and pleasing to God. "Now concerning virgins," says the same Apostle (Same), "I have no commandment of the Lord, but I give counsel, as having obtained mercy of the Lord to be faithful. . . . . . I would that all men were even as myself," that is to say, unmarried; "but every one has

3*

his proper gift from God, one after this manner, and another after that ; but I say to the unmarried and to the widows, it is good for them if they so continue, even as I. But if they do not contain themselves, let them marry ; for it is better to marry than to burn. . . . . If thou take a wife, thou hast not sinned ; and if a virgin marry, she hath not sinned ; nevertheless, such shall have tribulation of the flesh. . . . . Therefore, both he that giveth his virgin in marriage, doeth well ; and he that giveth her not, doeth better. . . . . . A woman is bound by the law as long as her husband liveth ; but if her husband die, she is at liberty ; let her marry to whom she will, only in the Lord. But more blessed shall she be if so she remain, according to my counsel ; and I think that I also have the Spirit of God."

This is the doctrine by which the church hath always been guided in strenuously defending, against the ancient heretics, the dignity of matrimony, and against the modern reformers, the supremacy of celibacy and virginity over the matrimonial state. Against the former, namely, the Manicheans, who, as Saint Paul says (1 Tim. 4), " giving heed to spirits of error and doctrines of devils, speaking lies in hypocrisy," were " forbidding to marry " as a diabolical institution, the church declared that matrimony is an institution of God, sanctified by our Lord, and raised by himself into the dignity of a sacrament under the Christian dispensation ; and against the latter, who, preferring matrimony to celibacy and virginity, not on account of the sacrament, which dignity they also denied to matrimony, but merely as something more congenial to them, and opposing celibacy, which they had vowed to God and were not

willing to keep, and therefore they condemned it, together with virginity, as contrary to their inclinations,
by which they measured the gospel truths, the church
declared, according to the above doctrine of our Lord
and his blessed Apostle, celibacy and virginity to be
preferable to matrimony, saying (Conc. Trin. Sess. 24,
Can. 10), " If any one say that the original state is to
be preferred to the state of virginity or celibacy, and
that it is not better and more blessed to live in virginity or celibacy than to contract matrimony, let him
be anathema."

According to this gospel's doctrine, blessed are they
who are called to the state of celibacy, whether male
or female, either to the ecclesiastical state or to the
state of a religious life, and persevere faithful to their
holy vocation. Such is the preëminence of celibacy
over matrimony, that when accompanied with solemn
vows in religion, even after a previous marriage contracted but not consummated, by virtue of the vows
the tie of matrimony is dissolved, so that the party
remaining in the world after the vows of the other
can contract matrimony with another. Whether this
be merely by virtue of the excellency of the religious
vows over matrimony, or by divine disposition in favor
of the religious life implied in that recommendation
made by Jesus Christ of renouncing all things, father,
mother, brother, sister, wife, and even one's life to
follow Him (Matt. c. 19, v. 29, Luke, c. 14, v. 26), or
lastly by virtue of a condition always implied in the
marriage contract, namely, " I contract for life, unless
previous to the consummation of matrimony I would
consecrate myself to God in religious life," certain it

is that matrimony contracted but not consummated is dissolved by solemn religious vows, as the church has declared according to the above said doctrine, condemning as heretics those who would dare to deny it: "If any one say . . . that matrimony contracted, but not consummated, is not dissolved by the solemn religious. profession of one of the contracting parties, let him be anathema." (Con. Trin. Sess. 24, Can. 6.) The reason of the dissolution of such marriage in favor of the more blessed state of religious life, is because the union of Jesus Christ with his church is fully represented and perfected only by consummation, by which the contracting parties become "one flesh," as also the members of the church, with relation to Christ, are said to be by the Apostle "of his flesh and of his bones" (Eph. c. 5, v. 30) ; and from said consummation results the absolute indissolubility of the matrimonial tie. Hence also comes the opinion of some divines, who affirm that the supreme pontiff, by virtue of the supreme power of the keys conferred on him by our Lord, can dissolve, in some extraordinary cases, the tie of said matrimony contracted, but not consummated ; and sustain their opinion by facts which prove the exercise of said power.

Returning to our subject, we say, according to the above said doctrine of our Lord, and that of the Apostle, that blessed are they who are called to a state of celibacy ; but, as all have not received this gift from God, so they are to be satisfied whom God hath called to a married life ; it is also a gift of God, although not so perfect ; they shall have tribulation of the flesh, as Saint Paul says. But they do well marrying when called ; and they shall find therein also, the means of sanctification and securing their eternal salvation, if they be faithful in complying with the duties thereof; in keeping, as the same Apostle says, the " Marriage honorable in all (things,) and the bed undefiled " (Heb. c. 13, v. 4) ; preserving, with the most assiduous diligence, the unity, perpetuity, and sanctity of the matrimonial state ; its unity by mutual fidelity ; its perpetuity by mutual society ; and its sanctity by mutual love and assistance. And these are the three duties resulting from the matrimonial engagement, which we are now going to explain.

In the first place, married persons are bound to preserve the unity of matrimony by mutual fidelity. From the moment they gave their mutual consent and engaged in matrimony, they delivered to each other their bodies, which are no more their own, but their companion's ; this made the Apostle say (1st Cor., c. 7) : " The wife hath not power over her own body, but the husband ; and in like manner the husband also hath not power of his own body, but the wife ;" and this is also the reason why, according to the same Apostle (Eph. c. 5, v. 28), " so also ought men to love their wives as their own bodies," and " he that loveth his wife, loveth himself ;" because " they are not two, but one flesh," as our Lord says. Hence, any one who is engaged in matrimony, whether male or female, who divides the love he owes to his companion with any other, toucheth at a forbidden fruit, rends the unity of matrimony, and becomes a practical " Mormonist," since there are more than two in one flesh, according to the doctrine of Saint Paul, saying : " know you not that he who adheres to a harlot, is made one body ? for they shall be," saith he, " two in one flesh." (1st Cor., c. 6, v. 16.) Who can comprehend the black injustice, and the awful consequences of this sin? often rendering uncertain the fruit of matrimonial engagements, and depriving the proper heirs of what property belongs to them, to give it to strangers. This is one of those monstrous deeds which should never be heard of amongst Christians; if in the ancient law they who were guilty of it, whether male or female, were ordered to be put to death, that the evil might be removed, for thus saith the Lord: "they shall both die," that is to say, the adulterer and the adulteress, "and thou shalt take away the evil out of Israel (Deut., c. 22, v. 22), what then must it be amongst Christians, whose bodies by baptism were made temples of God, and members of Christ! the Apostle saying: "know you not that your bodies are members of Christ? shall I then, taking the members of Christ, make them the members of a harlot? God forbid." * * "Know you not that your members are the temple of the Holy Ghost?" (1st Cor., c. 6, vv. 15, 19.)

God forbid that any Christian should so forget the unity of matrimony as to violate it by infidelity, for with such a foul crime he could not be admitted into the mansions of eternal bliss. Still it is not enough for married people to preserve unity by mutual fidelity. They must likewise preserve the perpetuity of their engagement by constant and mutual society, which obliges them to live together, united by the bond of family, according to the words of our Lord: "they are not two, but one flesh;" "what, therefore, God hath joined together, let not man put asunder." Saint Paul, who carefully explained all the duties of married persons, expresses this in the most clear and evident terms, saying (1st Cor., c. 7) : "to them that are married, not I, but the Lord commandeth that the wife depart not from her husband ; and if she depart, that she remain unmarried, or be reconciled to her husband. And let not the husband put away his wife." The very end and object of matrimony, namely, the procreation and proper education of children, imperatively demands that married people live in society together ; and they evidently violate this, God's commandment, who, to the great scandal of Christianity, live separated from one another ; which crime, as an abyss calleth for another abyss, often brings them to some other, even more grievous crime ; and the disregard for the perpetuity of marriage sometimes brings them to the violation of its unity; and the withdrawing from the path of Christianity carries them to that of "Mormonism."

Some reason had the Apostles then, when, hearing our Lord speak of the duties of married persons, said to him : " If the case of a man with his wife be so, it is not good to marry " (Matt., c. 19, v. 10) ; that is to say, it is better not to marry ; which declaration, as we have said, our Lord confirmed, celibacy being preferable to it, and a more blessed state ; for, as Saint Paul says, those that are married "shall have tribulation of the flesh " (1st Cor., c. 7) ; and such tribulation sometimes, that it becomes almost insupportable, the first affections having changed into antipathies, which daily increasing, at last convert the married state, from being a society of love into a society of hatred: into a hellish society. Oh ! how young people ought to reflect upon this before contracting matrimony, and be cautious in selecting a companion for life, being actuated not by flying passion and affection, but by the principles of religion and Christian prudence, in order not to expose themselves to the danger of perpetually bewailing their evil lot, and mixing their bitter tears and fruitless grief with their daily bread, as is the case with many an unfortunate couple. But is there no remedy to soothe and alleviate the unhappy lot of such as have been unfortunate in the selection of a companion, or whose dispositions have so changed after marriage, as to render his company unpleasant, painful, or even sometimes dangerous? or is an innocent victim to be always under the power of a tyrant, to be constantly immolated at the altar of anger? Does not religion offer some leniency to this, one of the greatest evils at this side of the grave? Yes; there is some remedy to this, afforded by religion, which alone can console when other remedies are unavailing. And first of all is the patience of Job, who in the midst of his heavy afflictions suffered the insults of his wife; and when this proves insufficient, then the Church, according to the doctrine of our Lord and His blessed Apostle, may allow, and even order a separation, or dissolution of family society, for a determined or undetermined time, as she may think best, according to circumstances, but retaining always firm the matrimonial contract until a reconciliation can be obtained; and those are condemned as heretics who refuse to the Church this power, and affirm that she errs in the exercise of it, saying: "If any one say that the Church errs, teaching that for many reasons a separation of the married couple for a certain or uncertain time, as to bed and cohabitation, can be commanded, let him be anathema.' (Con. Trid. Sess. 24; Can. 8.)

We need not dwell upon the different reasons or causes that may justify the dissolution of family society, for a time, as they may be many and various, depending on circumstances, rendering matrimonial society very unpleasant and insupportable. Saint Paul supposes them when he says (1st Cor. 7): "To them that are married, not I, but the Lord commandeth, that the wife depart not from her husband; and if she depart, that she remain unmarried, or be reconciled to her husband." Not any kind of reason, however, is sufficient for separation; nor is any of the parties concerned always the proper judge to decide when and where there is, or there is not sufficient cause for said separation, and thus declare that the Lord's commandment of cohabitation is, or is not binding on them any longer; this belongs to the Church and its pastors, the interpreters of God's holy law, and consequently of the duties resulting from matrimony, whose dispensation as a sacrament under the Christian Dispensation, exclusively belongs to them. To the Church, then, are the interested parties to apply for the proper decision. From these observations we understand how guilty they must be, who of their own authority, and for trivial reasons, separate, to the great scandal of Christian society, and often to the ruin of their own and their children's reputation.

There is nevertheless a crime for which, our Lord himself, notwithstanding the indissolubility of the marriage contract, allows to the innocent party, provided he has not been guilty of the same crime, to put away, and even forever, the monstrous companion. This is the crime of adultery; but without the liberty of marrying again to any other, which, as we said elsewhere, is only allowed in case of death. This is the doctrine of the Church according to that of our Lord (St. Matt., c. 5, v. 32): "I say to you, that whosoever shall put away his wife, excepting for the cause of fornication, causeth her to commit adultery; and whosoever shall marry her that is put away, committeth adultery." And again (c. 19, v. 9): "Whosoever shall put away his wife, except it be for fornication, and shall marry another, committeth adultery; and he who shall marry her that is put away, committeth adultery." We see here two things, namely, the liberty, for the innocent party, to put away the guilty monster for the cause of fornication; and the prohibition, for both, even for the innocent, to marry again to any other; since both the innocent and the criminal are said, by our Lord, to commit adultery if they marry to another. From this it appears evident that the crime of adultery, in either of the married couple, is a sufficient cause for separation, or dissolution of family society, in favor of the innocent, who has not given cause to it, nor has he been guilty of the same crime either before or after; in which case he could not claim any privilege over the other, the rights of matrimony being equal for both male and female, and where there are equal rights, there is also equal injustice, and a kind of compensation; although the crime be more grievous in the female, owing to the uncertainty of the matrimonial fruit and the right of inheritance, which might sometimes ensue.

The above said cause of adultery sets at liberty, as we have said, the innocent party, forever, of the matrimonial engagement, as to cohabitation and family society; so that he can withdraw from the companion of

his own authority, which the Lord gives him without
expecting the decision of the Church, provided he be
certain of the crime voluntarily and willfully committed;
and can enter even a religious life, and consecrate himself to God forever in religion; which he could not do
for any other cause, they being by their own nature
temporary, whilst the former is perpetual, making of
them more than "two in one flesh," contrary to God's
command; thus destroying as it were, what renders the
Christian matrimony so sacred and venerable, the union
of Jesus Christ with his church, which it represents.
This shows to married people what great care and
zeal they should have to preserve the unity of matrimony by mutual fidelity; the first duty resulting from
matrimonial engagement, and the most efficacious means
to preserve likewise its perpetuity by constant and mutual society of life, second duty of matrimony; and
thus it will also be a society of mutual love and assistance; third duty, and we might call it the reward of
their fidelity, by which they will preserve the sacredness and sanctity of the sacrament.

To them who fully comprehend the dignity and sanctity of matrimony, which is called by St. Paul " a great
sacrament . . . in Christ and in the church," it is easy
likewise to understand the duty of mutual love and
assistance resulting from it, which renders the yoke
really sweet and light, strengthens the unity of the
matrimonial engagement, confirms its perpetuity, and
forms the happiness of family society. It seems to us
that we can do nothing better in this respect than to
speak with, or rather quote the words of the Apostle to
the Ephesians (chap. 5), scarcely leave anything to be

added : "Let women," says he, "be subject to their husbands, as to the Lord ; because the husband is the head of the wife, as Christ is the head of the church ; He is the Saviour of his body. Therefore as the church is subject to Christ, so also let the wives be to their husbands in all things. Husbands, love your wives, as Christ also loved the church, and delivered himself up for it, that He might sanctify it, cleansing it by the laver of water in the word of life ; that He might present it to himself a glorious church, not having spot or wrinkle, nor any such thing, but that it should be holy and without blemish. So also ought men to love their wives as their own bodies. He that loveth his wife, loveth himself. For no man ever hated his own flesh, but nourisheth and cherisheth it, as also Christ doth the church ; for we are members of his body, of his flesh, and of his bones. For this cause shall a man leave his father and mother, and shall cleave to his wife, and they shall be two in one flesh. This is a great sacrament ; but I speak in Christ and in the church. Nevertheless, let every one of you in particular love his wife as himself, and let the wife reverence her husband." Thus far the Apostle, presenting before the eyes of the married people the union between Christ and his church, developing the admirable effects of said union, the unbounded charity of Jesus Christ for the church, and the untiring zeal of the church for the honor of her divine spouse, Jesus Christ ; and proposing the same as a model to them who, being called to the matrimonial state, are to be also a living figure and image of that great mystery of charity and love ; that being thus united by the bond of mutual affection and devotedness, they may have but one heart and one soul, as they are united in one flesh ; they may perpetually preserve their marriage "honorable in all things," by mutual fidelity, mutual society, and mutual affection, which will certainly bring them to that marriage feast where they shall be inebriated with the plenty of the house of God. (Psalms 35, v. 9.)